[Issued with Army Orders dated 1st October 1913.
[Crown copyright Reserved.

<u>OFFICIAL COPY</u>

REMOUNT MANUAL (WAR).

LONDON:
PRINTED UNDER THE AUTHORITY OF HIS MAJESTY'S STATIONERY OFFICE
BY HARRISON AND SONS, 45-47, ST. MARTIN'S LANE, W.C.,
PRINTERS IN ORDINARY TO HIS MAJESTY.

www.firesteppublishing.com

FireStep Editions

FireStep Publishing
Gemini House
136-140 Old Shoreham Road
Brighton
BN3 7BD

www.firesteppublishing.com

First published by the General Staff, War Office 1913.
First published in this format by FireStep Editions,
an imprint of FireStep Publishing, in association with
the National Army Museum, 2013.

NATIONAL ARMY MUSEUM

www.nam.ac.uk

ISBN 978-1-908487-75-9

Cover design FireStep Publishing
Typeset by FireStep Publishing
Printed and bound in Great Britain

Please note: *In producing in facsimile from original historical documents, any
imperfections may be reproduced and the quality may be lower than modern
typesetting or cartographic standards.*

OFFICIAL COPY.

[Issued with Army Orders dated 1st October, 1913.

[Crown Copyright Reserved.

116
Gen. No.
5533

REMOUNT MANUAL
(WAR).

LONDON:
PRINTED UNDER THE AUTHORITY OF HIS MAJESTY'S STATIONERY OFFICE
BY HARRISON AND SONS, 45-47, ST. MARTIN'S LANE, W.C.,
PRINTERS IN ORDINARY TO HIS MAJESTY.

To be purchased, either directly or through any Bookseller, from
WYMAN AND SONS, LTD., FETTER LANE, E.C., and 54, ST. MARY STREET, CARDIFF; or
H.M. STATIONERY OFFICE (SCOTTISH BRANCH), 23, FORTH STREET, EDINBURGH; or
E. PONSONBY, LTD., 116, GRAFTON STREET, DUBLIN;
or from the Agencies in the British Colonies and Dependencies,
the United States of America, the Continent of Europe and Abroad of
T. FISHER UNWIN, LONDON, W.C.

1913.

Price Two Pence.

This Manual is issued by command of the Army Council for the guidance of all concerned.

War Office,
 1st *October*, 1913.

EWD Ward

TABLE OF CONTENTS.

B 10536)   Wt. w. 22502-167   3500   10/13   H & S   P. 13/106

REMOUNT MANUAL (WAR).

The War Establishments (Part I), "Headquarters of administrative Services and Departments," gives details of officers of the remount service attached to headquarters in the field. Field Service Regulations, Part II, details the system under which remounts are supplied, and War Establishments gives the establishment of remount units.

Chapter I.—Organization and Duties of the Remount Service in the Field.

1.—*General description of the Remount Service.*

1. The remount service of an army in the field, under the orders of the C.-in-C. conveyed through the I.G.C., is organized and controlled by a Director of Remounts. It supplies remounts of all kinds for all services. (Field Service Regulations, Part II, Section 23.)

2. For a field army one remount depôt is usually required at each base, while advanced remount depôts are formed on the line of communication as may be necessary. (*See* War Establishments, Part I.)

3. Remount personnel does not normally proceed in advance of the advanced base, but on occasion "field remount sections" may be organized and detached from the advanced remount depôts. Their personnel may be found from the depôt or such source as may be most suitable.

4. It is a principle that horses and other animals admitted into veterinary hospitals are struck off the strength of the units to which they belong, and when sound become remounts being discharged to the nearest remount depôt.

5. It is also accepted that it is more economical to exchange debilitated animals for remounts, before they reach a stage of debility that will require many months to recover from.

6. Units normally arrive at the oversea base a little below the War Establishment of animals owing to casualties on the voyage and will only need the replacement of such casualties. Such casualties will be replaced from the advanced remount depôts (except as in para. 7).

7. The base remount depôt includes in the first instance among its riding horses, the first reinforcement for cavalry and mounted infantry.

8. Remounts are received at the base or other remount depôts from three sources, viz. :—

    (*a*) From outside the theatre of operations.

    (*b*) From purchase, capture, or requisition within the theatre of operations.

    (*c*) From veterinary hospitals.

9. The headquarters of the Director of Remounts and the advanced remount depôts, are among the earliest units to be sent to the base.

10. Remounts supplied from reserve units in the United Kingdom will normally arrive trained. The horses first allotted to the advanced and base remount depôts will probably have less training than those arriving later from reserve units.

A base remount depôt is provided with a proportion of personnel and equipment for remount training if necessary.

2.—*Territorial Force and Reserve Units.*

1. Units of the Territorial Force and all Reserve Formations, when at their war stations, are supplied with remounts from remount depôts in the United Kingdom.

3.—*Duties of the Remount Service in War.*

1. The duties of the remount service in war are briefly explained in Field Service Regulations, Part II. They include :—

    (*a*) The provision of the wants of the army in remounts, and the formulation of demands on the military authorities concerned.

    (*b*) The receipt of all animals from outside the theatre of operations.

    (*c*) The purchase of animals locally.

    (*d*) The disposal of captured or requisitioned animals.

    (*e*) The issue of remounts to the army, in accordance with orders from the I.G.C., fit for work, trained, shod up, sound, and in good wind.

2. The purchase of remounts outside the theatre of war is not normally the duty of the remount service in the field, and is controlled by the military authorities of the Government directing the campaign.

3. The training of remounts is not usually a duty of the remount service in the field, except as regards animals obtained locally.

CHAPTER II.—DUTIES OF SENIOR AND DETACHED OFFICERS.

4.—*Director of Remounts.*

1. The duties of the Director of Remounts are defined in Field Service Regulations, Part II, Section 23. He advises on all technical matters connected with his service, and subject to the instructions of the C.-in-C. (or of the I.G.C., Field Service Regulations, Part II, Section 11), controls all arrangements in connection with it. He administers the personnel of the service in question, for the distribution of which he is responsible. (Field Service Regulations, Part II, Section 22–2.) He is responsible for the economical administration of horses generally.

2. The Director of Remounts will normally be with the headquarters of the I.G.C., subject to the provision of Field Service Regulations, Part II, Section 22-7, which says, "The offices of directors and heads of administrative services and departments will be located as directed from time to time by the C.-in-C. When a director accompanies general headquarters a deputy will usually be on the L. of C. and *vice versa*."

3. The provision of remounts includes the forwarding of timely forecasts of the army's requirements to the authority supplying remounts from outside the theatre of war.

4. In accordance with the general principles defined in Field Service Regulations, Part II, Section 22, the administration of the remount service includes the control of such remount units as are in the field, with the control of the personnel of the service, and, under instruction from the I.G.C., the distribution and organization of the service on the lines of communication by areas, districts, or sections, as required.

The Director of Remounts must bring to notice or advise the Q.M.G's branch of the staff on :—

(*a*) The location of remount depôts generally.

(*b*) The need for training establishments for horses, if those normally provided in the base remount depôt are insufficient.

(*c*) The need for, and size of any rest depôts for convalescent horses, that may appear necessary.

(*d*) The need for any advanced or base depôts in excess of those originally provided for the force.

(*e*) The need for the temporary formation of "field remount sections" in advance of the advanced base.

5.—*Duties of Deputy and Assistant Directors.*

1. The duties of the deputy director normally attached to general headquarters are as follows :—

(*a*) To keep the staff informed of remount arrangements generally.

(b) To keep the Director of Remounts cognisant of the general trend of operations.

2. The duties of the A.D.R. in charge of the remount service on the L. of C. are :—

(a) To control the remount service of the L. of C. in accordance with the plans of the D. of R.
(b) To supervise the work of the depôts.
(c) To carry out any additional remount duties that may arise.
(d) To authorize the destruction of unfit horses in remount depôts and depute such authority when desirable.

3. Should the L. of C. or theatre of operations be sub-divided into remount sections or areas, the remount officer in charge will carry out duties similar to those of the A.D.R. and under his general control, for the area to which he is appointed.

4. The duties of the senior remount officer at the base are :—

(a) To supervise all remount depôts at the base.
(b) To arrange for the receipt of arrivals in accordance with orders from base headquarters.
(c) To advise on, and assist in, the formation of horse farms and rest depôts necessary at the base should circumstances render such necessary. (Personnel must be drawn from the remount service unless the C.-in-C. has approved other arrangements, necessitated by exceptional circumstances.)

5. All remount officers in charge of areas and depôts must keep the A.D.R. informed of their requirements.

CHAPTER III.—REMOUNT UNITS.

6.—*Functions of Depôts.*

1. In general the function of the depôts is to feed units of the army with animals and one another in personnel and animals, and similarly to relieve one another of inefficients.* They may also be required to issue direct to troops detached from the main armies. Every care will be taken to prevent the infection of remount depôts by the introduction into them of diseased animals. The reception and treatment of such animals is the function of the veterinary service, and animals requiring treatment will not be received into remount depôts.

2. The personnel of the depôts will be expanded by local labour when required, under the orders of the I.G.C. or Base Commandant, and in emergency the nearest commander may be asked for temporary aid.

---

* *i.e.* Horses not sufficiently fit or conditioned for work apart from those actually sick.

3. *The base remount depôt* is a stationary unit at which all the functions of a remount depôt, in classification, training and recuperation can be completed and carried out. This is the principal source of supply to the front, and should be kept full. It is essential that there should be plenty of room for the various sections.

4. A separate roomy and sufficiently distant section of the base depôt will be required as the operations develop, for the purpose of receiving from the advanced remount depôts, horses requiring prolonged rest, which are not detained in veterinary hospitals, and convalescents discharged from veterinary hospitals. It may become necessary to form similar sections, organized as special depôts and convalescent farms, at various suitable places, where forage is plentiful, on the L. of C. (when separate from the base depôt ; these are termed "rest depôts"). The provision of personnel for these, if it cannot be spared from the base remount depôt, will be a matter of arrangement at the time by the C.-in-C. Acclimatization may also require the establishment of special sections or depôts.

5. *Advanced remount depôts* are pushed up along the L. of C. to feed the army with horses. They are maintained at their normal strength of fit horses by constant drafts from the base. They receive all convalescent or captured horses free from disease that may be handed them, and will evacuate to the depôts in rear those animals unlikely to become available for early issue.

6. The *field remount sections* that may from time to time be formed temporarily, perform the same functions as advanced remount depôts.

7. Field remount sections must be cleared of unfit horses immediately.

8. All depôts other than field remount sections (when formed) should be organized by sections as follows :—

   (*a*) Fit for immediate use.
   (*b*) Temporary detention.
   (*c*) Prolonged rest either at the base or other rest depôt.

Horses in category (*b*) and (*c*) will, unless advanced depôts have rest depôts attached, be constantly transferred down the L. of C.

7.—*Internal organization of Depôts.*

1. The organization of a depôt on first landing or reaching destination will vary considerably from its more settled form. On arrival, the first need is to arrange for prompt picketing or other accommodation for animals in fields or paddocks pending a more permanent arrangement. As soon as time permits the "Kraal" system will be introduced, as explained in Appendix IV, either for the depôt as a whole, or for each of its sections. It may be possible to have the kraals arranged before the arrival of the depôts.

2. *The base remount depôt*, will normally consist of a headquarters and three sections, with the distribution of personnel and horses as shown in Appendix I. Nos. 1 and 2 sections will be for riding horses, and No. 2 for draught horses.

3. This depôt is a large unit and circumstances may require that its sections shall be separated, or that only a portion of the horses may be on lines, and the remainder in fields and paddocks till the kraals are made. Conditions referred to in section 6, para. 4, may demand a redistribution of personnel before many weeks have elapsed since the landing of the depôt.

4. It is important to exercise the horses for immediate issue under saddle, and for this purpose a considerable riding personnel is available ; while the paddocks and exercise courses for unridden animals must be provided as soon as possible. The "kraal" system keeps animals in a hard condition with a minimum of personnel.

5. The routine to be followed in each depôt must depend on circumstances, and standing orders must be issued at once. A *precis* as a basis of standing orders, is given in Appendix III.

6. The armed personnel of remount depôts is available to take part in local defence schemes, and suitable alarm posts must be organized.

CHAPTER IV.—ADMINISTRATIVE DETAILS.

8.—*Issue of Remounts.*

1. Instructions will be received from the I.G.C. in case of exceptional demands, as to the authority required for the issue of remounts, as priority can only be decided by high authority. (Field Service Regulations, Part II, Section 26 (10).)

2. Remounts will, however, in the absence of other orders, be issued to units on demand (*see* Field Service Regulations, Part II, Sec. 79–4). The section also provides for the divisional commander being kept informed of demands made by units. When remounts available are less than requirements, depôt commanders must take the orders of the D. of R. *re* priority.

3. Officers who may indent for horses for their own use are responsible for the propriety of their demand, and depôt commanders will comply with such demands when in their power.

4. Horses will only be issued to press correspondents on the orders of general headquarters or the I.G.C.

5. The minimum strength necessary for road conducting parties is as follows :—

1 Officer   per 100 horses ⎱ The remount unit can not normally
1 Serjeant   „   50   „   ⎰ furnish these parties, which must
1 Soldier   „   3   „   ⎰ be arranged for by the I.G.C.

6. Rail conducting parties between base and advanced remount depôts will be found by the remount service, in proportion of 1 soldier or horse-keeper per 2 trucks, and 1 N.C.O. per 15 men.

7. Captured animals are usually disposed of as directed in Field Service Regulations, Part II.

9.—*Reports and Returns.*

1. Since all units in the field are maintained at War Establishment, no returns of the horses with units are necessary, as the demands that come in are sufficient indication of any deficiencies.

2. A ledger will be maintained in each depôt showing receipts and issues of animals by classes on Army Form A 2045. These accounts will include, on the receipt side, animals as under :—

    (i) Consigned to the depôts from overseas, or otherwise.
    (ii) Transferred from units of the army.
    (iii) Purchased locally.
    (iv) Requisitioned, captured, or found straying.

On the issue side of the account entries will be made, supported by vouchers, showing how the animals, as above, have been disposed of.

3. A manuscript return from each depôt will be posted to the Director of Remounts, each day, showing the numbers of animals in the depôt, to be rendered in the form given in Appendix II. Any further reports considered necessary, will be ordered by the Director of Remounts as required.

4. Remount accounts* will be rendered at the end of each month to the Director of Remounts, supported by vouchers. These accounts will be transmitted to the Command Paymaster for audit in due course.

5. During active operations stock will be taken from time to time, as circumstances permit, by officers specially deputed for the purpose, of the animals at depôts, and any discrepancies will be brought to the notice of the Director of Remounts.

6. The necessary facilities will be given to the Army Pay Department to enable them to carry out their audit of accounts.

7. The ordinary army returns and accounts to be rendered are detailed in Field Service Regulations, Part II.

CHAPTER V.—PURCHASE OF REMOUNTS.

10.—*General Rules for Purchase.*

1. The purchase of remounts will normally be carried out under the Rules for Requisitioning as laid down in Field Service Regulations, Part II, Chap. VI. This manual will govern the purchase of all animals within the theatre of operations, or within the jurisdiction of the Director of Remounts in the field, whether the animals are purchased by requisition or in the open market. Purchase in the open market will depend on the orders of the C.-in-C.

2. The duties of purchasing will ordinarily be carried out by officers of the remount service, but if these are not available the Director of Remounts may have to report that the service cannot be carried on unless temporary assistance can be afforded.

---

* Viz., Animal and Store Account.

3. The personnel required to assist purchasers will be detailed from the remount service.

4. All animals purchased in the field will be sent to the nearest remount depôt unless other specific orders have been given. If conducting parties are necessary and have not been provided for, the purchaser must inform the Director of Remounts, if the nearest commander cannot give temporary assistance.

5. A report of purchases made will be submitted weekly to the Director of Remounts.

11.—*Purchase Accounts.*

1. Should it be necessary to resort to cash purchase, the Director of Remounts will request the Paymaster-in-Chief to arrange for the necessary imprests, informing that officer of the names of the purchasing officers, amounts to be issued to each, and locality. He will at the same time furnish the Paymaster-in-Chief with specimens of the purchasing officer's signature in duplicate. The Paymaster-in-Chief will inform him to which field paymaster the order to issue has been sent. Any further imprests will be obtained in the same way.

2. Army Form N 1531 A in respect of these imprests will be rendered to the Command Pay Office at the base through the Director of Remounts, who will endorse the cash account to the effect that the animals purchased have been duly added to the effective strength of the army in the field. All charges will be supported by the receipt of the payee or other proof of payment.

APPENDIX I.

TABLE SHOWING THE DISTRIBUTION OF A BASE REMOUNT DEPÔT CONSISTING OF A HEADQUARTERS AND THREE SECTIONS.

	Head-quarters.	No. 1 Section (Riding Horses).	No. 2 Section (Riding Horses).	No. 3 Section (Draught Horses).	Total.
Commandant	1	—	—	—	1
Assistant Commandant ...	1	—	—	—	1
Remount Officers	2 (a)	3	3	3	9
Adjutant	1	—	—	—	1
Quartermaster	1	—	—	—	1
Ridingmasters	—	—	—	—	—
Veterinary Officers	3	—	—	—	3
Warrant Officer (S.M.) ...	1	—	—	—	1
Company Serjeant-Major ...	1	1	1	1	4
„ Qr.-Master-Serjt....	1	1	1	1	4
Serjeants	4 (b)	4	4	4	16
Farrier Qr.-Master-Serjt. ...	—	1	—	—	1
„ Staff-Serjeants ...	—	2	3	3	8
„ Serjeants	—	—	—	—	—
Shoeing-Smith-Corporals ...	—	—	—	—	—
Shoeing-Smiths	—	16	17	17	50
Saddler-Corporals	1	1	—	—	2
Saddlers...	—	1	2	2	5
Trumpeters	1	—	—	—	1
Corporals	3 (c)	7	7	7	24
Privates...	102 (d)	216	216	216	750
Batmen	9	3	3	3	18
Horses { Riding	—	875	875	—	—
Horses { Draught	—	—	—	850	—

(a) To superintend riding.   (b) 2 riders, 2 clerks.

(c) Riders.   (d) 100 riders, 2 clerks.

APPENDIX II.

———

Return of Animals in the Remount Depôt at...

on...

	Horses.						Mules.	Total.
	R. 1.	R. 2.	L.D. 1.	L.D. 2.	H.D.	P.		
Fit for issue ...								
Unfit for issue ...								
Total ...								

Commanding Remount Depôt.

(Date)

R. 1 = Cavalry.   R. 2 = Cobs.   L.D. 1 = Artillery.
L.D. 2 = Transport.   H.D. = Heavy Draught.   P. = Pack.

APPENDIX III.

———

Precis of Standing Orders for a Remount Depôt—

1. Standing Orders naturally vary between a depôt in which horses are stabled or picketted, and in a depôt in which all horses are in kraals. (This being the normal system at the base.)

2. Standing Orders must provide for—

  (i) *General routine—*

    (*a*) Organization of depôt.
    (*b*) Reception stable.
    (*c*) Sick lines.
    (*d*) Alarm post.
    (*e*) Sick men.

  (ii) *Stable routine—*

    (*a*) Normal hours of feeding—and hay up—exercise and water.
    (*b*) Orders *re* rugging.
    (*c*) Special feeds, such as weekly mashes.
    (*d*) Number and duties of stablemen.
    (*e*) Hours of stables.

  (iii) *Kraals.*

When the depôt has been organized on the kraal system.

    (*a*) As in (*a*) (*c*) and (*d*) above, with orders *re* clearing of each kraal for exercise.

  (iv) *Sick animals—*

    (*a*) Orders *re* reporting sick, transfer to sick lines.

  (v) *Issues—*

    (*a*) Normal procedure—and conducting parties.
    (*b*) Responsibility for despatch and entraining.

  (vi) *Receipt—*

    (*a*) Normal procedure—and conducting parties.
    (*b*) Reception.

APPENDIX IV.

THE KRAAL SYSTEM.

A.—*The internal arrangement of a depôt.*

1. On first opening a remount depôt it may be necessary to picket the horses (breast-high lines being used wherever possible), but their handling then involves great labour. The important point in a War Remount depôt is to issue horses fit for work, and, since there are many calls on the personnel, to do the same with as few men as possible.

2. To attain this object every depôt, or every section of a depôt, if isolated, must be arranged as soon as possible on the kraal system, as explained below, which is equally suitable for any number of horses, and can be improvised in existing fields or enclosures, or specially erected on some open space.

3. By this system the horses are kept fit for work and in natural health and condition with little or no grooming.

4. The plan should include a railed oval exercising track, A.A. (*see* Fig. I), surrounded by a number of paddocks, connected with it by gates. The paddocks, B.B., may be of varying size, and each should contain horses of varying classes and stages of fitness. Each section of a Base Remount Depôt should have a set of these paddocks to itself, all adjoining the same track. Attached to the track should be a water kraal, C, and a shunt kraal, D. In large depôts water will be laid on to troughs in each kraal, where possible.

On one portion of the track a crush is made, E.E., with raised footway, F.F., and swing block door, G.

5. *Working the system.*—To work the system (the kraals being full of loose horses) at the appointed daily hour, the gate from No. 1 kraal into the track is opened, and the horses, perhaps 200 in number, are let into the track and kept moving round for half an hour, or less—a very few men will do this. When exercise is over, the leading horses are diverted at J into the water kraal, C, where all the rest will follow and stop to drink. While the horses are on the track, the feeds are put into the troughs in the empty kraal and hay arranged round the sides. The horses of No. 1 kraal, now healthily warm, are drinking, and No. 2's horses are let in the track. When No. 1 has watered, they are turned into the shunt kraal, D. When No. 2 horses are let into the water kraal, No. 1 horses from the shunt kraal are let back into their own kraal *via* the track. As soon as the track is clear again, No. 3 horses are let into it, and so on. This should take place at least twice a day. It will be noticed how very few attendants are thus required for a very large number of horses. It will also be noticed how an observer at X can see all the horses from a kraal as they pass him.

6. *The crush.*—The crush, E.E., is an important part of the system. By its means each horse can be passed slowly in review, a headstall put on any required, by men standing on the raised footway, F.F., and horses led quietly away for shoeing, issue, etc. The block doorway, G, prevents a horse rushing from the crush, and the hurdle, H, makes him turn, and easy to hold if inclined to be unmanageable (*see* also Figure 2). Loose hurdles may be necessary to turn horses into the crush when required, and should be kept handy to each kraal gate also, but every effort should be made to induce horses to do things of their own accord and to avoid driving.

Fig. II

Swing Gate G, with cross end to close crush.

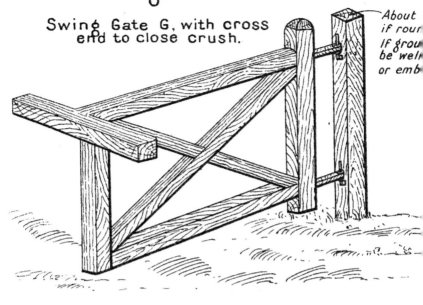

About
if rour
If grou
be weln
or emb

Plan

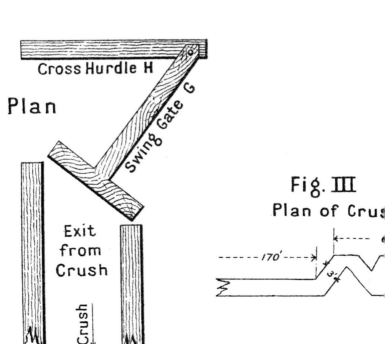

Cross Hurdle H

Swing Gate G

Exit from Crush

Crush

Fig. III
Plan of Crus

- - - - 170' - - - →

RAAL SYSTEM

or 9" diameter
nk 3' into ground.
t, the post should
ck to an anchorage,
some concrete.

Fig. I

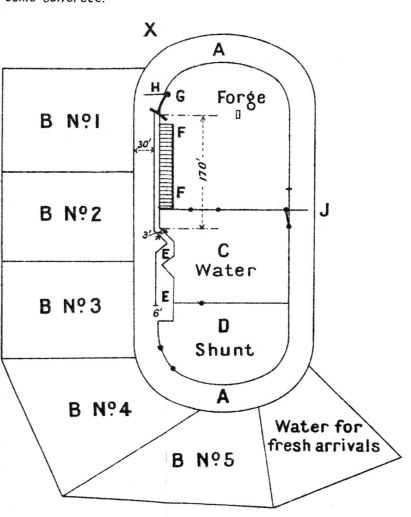

The dimensions of the Kraals (B) and the length
and breadth of the Oval, must vary according
to circumstances. The length of the track should
be from 400 to 600 Yards.

INDEX.